CATS

A Feline Potpourri

Ariel Books

Andrews and McMeel • Kansas City

10 9

ISBN: 0-8362-3002-7

Library of Congress Catalog Card Number:
91-77106

Book design by Judith A. Stagnitto

Table of Contents

CATS

A Feline Potpourri

Introduction

Cats are a paradox. From the time of the Pharaohs, their unique character has inspired both worship and awe. For while there is nothing so comforting as the purr of a contented cat, there always lingers the impression that it is you who is there for it. Cats always seem to have the upper hand.

Of course, any animal this fascinating will be written about—the cat has practically gathered its own literature. Great wits and writers, poets and politicians, cat owners and others have had their say about these remarkable creatures. And yet the feline always emerges unexplained and unimpressed.

Gathered here are some of the best attempts at capturing the essence of the cat. Poems, quotations, selections from literature, and myths—all directed at that fuzzy riddle that shares our laps and our lives.

Cats in History

The first domesticated cats were, of course, worshipped as gods.

The Egyptians first opened their houses to cats, where they were honored as representatives of the gods. The first Egyptian cat-god was Mafdet, who reigned from 2500 to 2280 B.C. The Egyptian sky goddess, Nut, was often depicted with the head of a cat, and the sun god, Ra, was often referred to as the Great Cat. The most famous cat-goddess was Bast, goddess of fire and the moon. The city of Bubastis was dedicated to her, its temples filled with cats tended by a special group of priestesses. Each spring 700,000 worshippers attended the festival of Bast, held in the city.

The Egyptians, naturally enough, tried to keep their divine felines entirely to themselves. It was illegal to export a cat from ancient Egypt. Legend has it that in 1500 B.C., a group of Greek traders smuggled about a dozen cats from Egypt, bred them, and began a trade in cats throughout the ancient world. By the first century A.D., they were common pets in the ancient world, and the custom of keeping a house cat was spread by the Romans throughout northern Europe as well.

In China, house cats were common from about 400 A.D. on. The Chinese considered cats a symbol of peace, fortune, and family serenity. In Japan, cats were so highly valued that they were not allowed to run free; cat owners kept their pets on silk leashes. When, in the seventeenth century, rats and mice seriously damaged granaries and all but destroyed the silk industry, the Japanese emperor decreed that all cats should be allowed to run free. Soon, the Japanese cats had the pests under control, and the Japanese economy was saved.

Several centuries earlier, in the West, cats had played a more historic role. In fact, it's no exaggeration to say that cats played an important role in saving European civilization!

In Europe's Dark Ages, bigotry and

ignorance had led to the persecution of cats, since their mysterious and inscrutable ways had identified them with Satan in the popular imagination. By the end of the fourteenth century, the European house cat had almost disappeared.

That same century, ships bringing Crusaders from the Middle East also brought some uninvited guests—rats carrying the bubonic plague. The Black Death struck Europe, and nearly half the population died. Although it was impossible to control the disease when it struck, it was possible to check the carrier of the disease—with cats. Europeans began once more to welcome them into their homes. It was cats' keen hunting abilities that saved them—and Europeans—from extinction.

Cats are still loved and worshipped by their owners. The same qualities that made them objects of terror in more superstitious times now enthrall us.

Cats have inspired poets and painters, writers and thinkers. They have even given rise to musicals. Other pets may also win our love and devotion, but few animals have earned the respect we pay the cat. Perhaps it is because, unlike other pets, they don't seem to need us as much as we need them.

A Feline Potpourri

Cat Quotations

Cats are mysterious beings. . . . You never know if they love you or if they condescend to occupy your house. This mystery is what makes them the most attractive beast.

PAUL MOORE

Ye shall not possess any beast, my dear sisters, except only a cat.

THE ANCREN RIEWLE
(NUN'S RULE)

Like those great sphinxes lounging
through eternity in noble attitudes upon
the desert sand, they gaze incuriously at
nothing, calm and wise.

CHARLES BAUDELAIRE

Our perfect companions never have fewer
than four feet.

COLETTE

If you want to know the character of a
man, find out what his cat thinks of him.

ANONYMOUS

At whiles it seems as if one were
somewhat as the cats, which ever have
appeared to me to be animals of two
parts, the one of the house and the
cushion and the prepared food, the other
that is free of the night and runs wild
with the wind in its coat and the smell of
the earth in its nostrils.

UNA L. SILBERRAD

The cat loves fish but does not like to wet her paws.

ENGLISH PROVERB

Cats seem to go on the principle that it never does any harm to ask for what you want.

JOSEPH WOOD KRUTCH

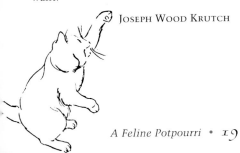

A Feline Potpourri • 19

No matter how much the cats fight, there always seem to be plenty of kittens.

ABRAHAM LINCOLN

All animals are equal, but some animals are more equal than others.

GEORGE ORWELL

Cats are rather delicate creatures and they are subject to a good many different ailments, but I never heard of one who suffered from insomnia.

JOSEPH WOOD KRUTCH

There is one respect in which brutes show real wisdom when compared with us—I mean their quiet, placid enjoyment of the present moment.

ARTHUR SCHOPENHAUER

Of all God's creatures there is only one
that cannot be made the slave of the lash.
That one is the cat. If man could be
crossed with the cat it would improve
man, but it would deteriorate the cat.

MARK TWAIN

God made the cat in order that man
might have the pleasure of caressing the
lion.

FERNAND MERY

Confront a child, a puppy, and a kitten
with a sudden danger; the child will turn
instinctively for assistance, the puppy
will grovel in abject submission . . . the
kitten will brace its tiny body for a frantic
resistance.

SAKI

The best thing about animals is that they
don't talk much.

THORNTON WILDER

From the dawn of creation the cat has known his place, and he has kept it, practically untamed and unspoiled by man. He has retinue. Of all animals, he alone attains to the Contemplative Life. He regards the wheel of existence from without, like the Buddha. There is no pretense of sympathy about the cat. He lives alone, aloft, sublime, in a wise passiveness. . . .

ANDREW LANG

Dogs come when they're called; cats take
a message and get back to you.

MARY BLY

Cats are smarter than dogs. You can't get
eight cats to pull a sled through snow.

JEFF VALDEZ

A Feline Potpourri

You have now learned to see
That cats are much like you and me
And other people whom we find
Possessed of various types of mind.

T. S. ELIOT

I think that the reason that we admire cats, those of us who do, is their proficiency in one-upmanship. They always seem to come up on top, no matter what they are doing—or pretend to be doing. . . . Maybe we secretly envy them.

BARBARA WEBSTER

The playful kitten, with its pretty little tigerish gambols, is infinitely more amusing than half the people one is obliged to live with in the world.

LADY SYDNEY MORGAN

I've met many thinkers and many cats, but the wisdom of cats is infinitely superior.

HIPPOLYTE TAINE

Animals are not brethren, they are not underlings; they are other nations, caught with ourselves in the net of life and time.

HENRY BESTON

Animals are such agreeable friends—they ask no questions; they pass no criticisms.

GEORGE ELIOT

The Bookish Cat

From The Cat That Walked by Himself

He will kill Mice and he will be kind to Babies when he is in the house, as long as they do not pull his tail too hard. But when he has done that, and between times, he is the Cat that walks by himself and all places are alike to him, and if you look out at nights you can see him waving his wild tail and walking by his wild lone—just the same as before.

RUDYARD KIPLING

From La Ménagerie Intime

It is no easy task to win the friendship of a cat. He is a philosopher, sedate, tranquil, a creature of habit, a lover of decency and order. He does not bestow his regard lightly, and, though he may consent to be your companion, he will never be your slave. Even in his most affectionate moods he preserves his freedom, and refuses a servile obedience. But once gain his confidence, and he is a friend for life. He shares your hours of work, of solitude, of melancholy. He

spends whole evenings on your knee,
purring and dozing, content with your
silence, and spurning for your sake the
society of his kind.

THÉOPHILE GAUTIER

The Pope's Cat

I have as companion a big greyish-red cat
with black stripes across it. It was born in
the Vatican, in the Raphael loggia. Leo XII
brought it up in a fold of his robes where I
had often looked at it enviously when the
Pontiff gave me an audience. . . . It was
called "the Pope's cat." In this capacity, it
used to enjoy the special consideration of
pious ladies. I am trying to make it forget
exile, the Sistine Chapel, the sun on

Michelangelo's cupola, where it used to walk, far above the earth.

VICOMTE DE
CHATEAUBRIAND

Untitled

Such is one of those big-whiskered and
well-furred tom-cats, that you see quiet in
a corner, digesting at his leisure, sleeping
if it seems good to him, sometimes giving
himself to the pleasure of hunting, for the
rest enjoying life peaceably, without
being troubled by restless reflections, and
little caring to communicate his thoughts
to others. Truly it needs only that a
female cat come on the scene to derange

all his philosophy; but are our
philosophers any wiser on such
occasions?

FATHER BOUGEANT

Dr. Johnson's Hodge

I shall never forget the indulgence with
which he treated Hodge, his cat; for
whom he used to go out and buy oysters,
lest the servants having that trouble
should take a dislike to the poor creature.
. . . I recollect him one day scrambling up
on Dr. Johnson's breast, apparently with
much satisfaction, while my friend,
smiling and half-whistling, rubbed his
back and pulled him by the tail; and
when I observed he was a fine cat, saying,
"Why, yes, Sir, but I have had cats whom

I liked better than this." And then as if perceiving Hodge to be out of countenance adding, "But he is a very fine cat, very fine cat indeed."

JAMES BOSWELL

41

A Letter From Samuel Clemens (Mark Twain)

Redding, Connecticut,
October 2, 1908

Dear Mrs. Patterson,

The contents of your letter are very pleasant and very welcome, and I thank you for them, sincerely. If I can find a photograph of my "Tammany" and her kittens, I will enclose it in this. One of them likes to be crammed into a corner pocket of the billiard table—which he fits as snugly as does a finger in a glove and then he watches the game (and obstructs it) by the hour, and spoils many a shot by putting out his paw and changing the direction of a passing ball. Whenever a ball is in his arms, or so close to him that it cannot be played upon without risk of hurting him, the player is privileged to remove it to any one of the 3 spots that chances to be vacant. . . .

SINCERELY YOURS,
S. L. CLEMENS

The Mysterious Cat

Some Cat Superstitions

Black cats were traditionally considered
unlucky in the United States; in England
it was white cats that were thought to
bring bad luck.

In Canada, three-colored cats were
considered unlucky.

The Japanese thought calico cats brought luck.

The Chinese believed that the older and uglier a cat was, the more good fortune it would bring.

Northern Europeans thought it brought bad luck if a cat crossed your path from the left, but it was good luck if a cat crossed from right to left. And it was especially fortunate if a cat entered a house of its own will.

According to folklore in the southern United States, a cat could predict the weather. If she washed behind her ears, winked, or sneezed once, it meant rain. If she ran about in a frenzy, it meant high winds were coming. If she sat with her backside to the fire, it meant frosty weather was on its way.

And the Indonesians thought they could cause rain by pouring water on a cat.

Cat Lore

From Bibliotheke

Whoever kills a cat in Egypt is condemned to death, whether he committed this crime deliberately or not. The people gather and kill him. An unfortunate Roman, who had accidentally killed a cat, could not be saved, either by King Ptolemy of Egypt or by the fear which Rome inspired.

DIODORUS SICULUS

How to Change into a Cat

Isobel Gowdie, a confessed Scottish witch who was burned in 1665, revealed the spell used to change into a cat and to change back again. Each incantation should be repeated three times.

To change into a cat:

I shall goe intill ane catt,
With sorrow, and sych, and a blak shott;
And I sall goe in the Divellis nam,
Ay will I com hom againe.

To change back into a human:

Catt, catt, God send thee a blak shott.
I am in a cattis liknes just now,
Bot I sal be in a womanis liknes ewin
now.
Catt, catt, God send thee a blak shott.

The Kitten at Play

See the kitten on the wall,
Sporting with the leaves that fall,
Withered leaves, one, two, and three
Falling from the elder tree,
Through the calm and frosty air
Of the morning bright and fair.

See the kitten, how she starts,
Crouches, stretches, paws and darts;
With a tiger-leap half way
Now she meets her coming prey.

Lets it go as fast and then
Has it in her power again.

Now she works with three and four,
Like an Indian conjurer;
Quick as he in feats of art,
Gracefully she plays her part;
Yet were gazing thousands there;
What would little Tabby care?

WILLIAM WORDSWORTH

63

Some cats is blind,
And stone-deaf some,
But ain't no cat
Wuz ever dumb.

ANTHONY HENDERSON
EUWER

Grave scholars and mad lovers all admire
And love, and each alike, at his full tide
Those suave and puissant cats, the
   fireside's pride,
Who like the sedentary life and glow of
   fire.

CHARLES BAUDELAIRE

A Feline Potpourri • 65

Stately, kindly, lordly
friend condescend
Here to sit by me,
and turn
Glorious eyes that smile
and burn. . . .

ALGERNON CHARLES
SWINBURNE

From A Poet's Lamentation for the Loss
of His Cat

Whene'er I felt my towering fancy fail,
I stroked her head, her ears, her tail,
And, as I stroked, improved my dying
     song
From the sweet notes of her melodious
     tongue.
Her purrs and mews so evenly kept time,
She purred in metre and she mewed in
     rhyme.

JOSEPH GREEN

On a Cat Ageing

He blinks upon the hearth-rug
And yawns in deep content,
Accepting all the comforts
That Providence has sent.

Louder he purrs and louder,
In one glad hymn of praise
For all the night's adventures,
For quiet, restful days.

Life will go on forever,
With all that cat can wish;

Warmth, and the glad procession
Of fish and milk and fish.

Only—the thought disturbs him—
He's noticed once or twice,
That times are somehow breeding
A nimbler race of mice.

SIR ALEXANDER GRAY